When we look up into the night sky, the Moon is the biggest thing we can see. In fact, the Moon is smaller than the Earth. The Moon looks so big because it is not as far away as the stars and other planets.

There are nine planets that go around or "orbit" the Sun.

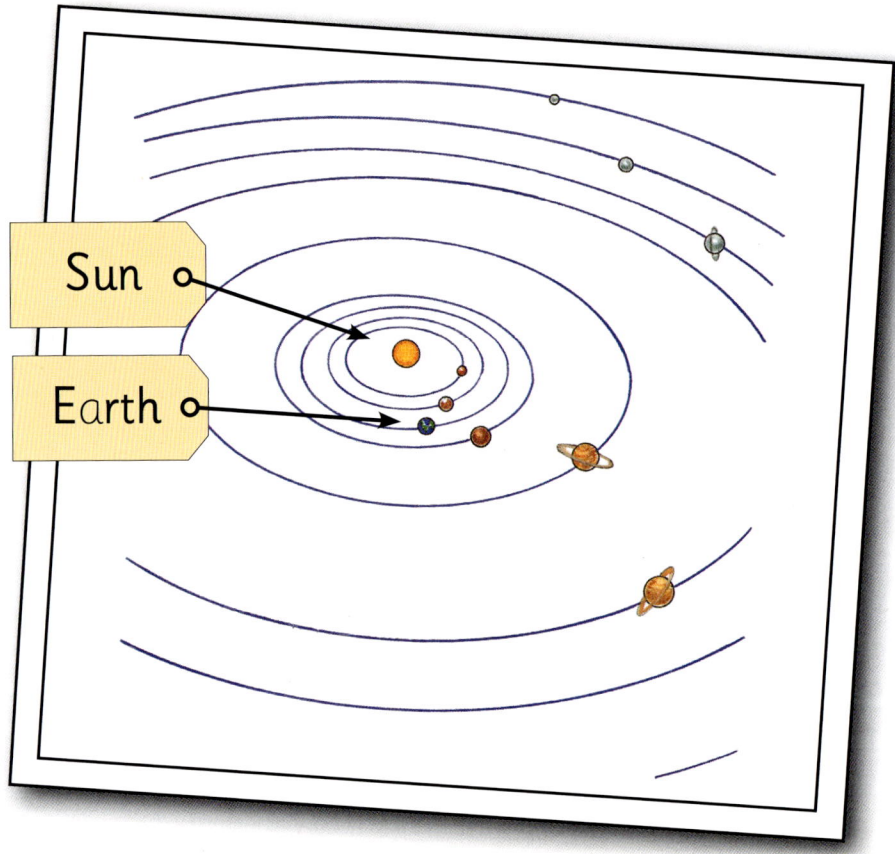

Earth, the planet we live on, is one of those planets. It is the third planet from the Sun.

The Moon orbits the Earth and, at the same time, it spins around too. It takes about 28 days for the Moon to spin around, and also for it to go around the Earth.

Astronomers look at the Moon and stars and planets. Today, they have big telescopes that let them see things that are a long way away. The first astronomers did not have such good telescopes for studying the Moon.

telescope

plain

When you look at the Moon, you can see dark and light patches on it. The first astronomers mistook the dark patches for seas. They named them things like The Sea of Clouds and The Sea of Tranquility. The Moon does not have any seas. The dark patches are big, flat bits of ground called plains.

It looks as if the Moon shines down on the Earth but, in fact, the Moon does not have any light of its own. It looks like it shines because it reflects the light from the Sun.

The Moon is always round. But sometimes it looks as if it is a different shape. This is because we can only see the part of the Moon that is in the light of the Sun.

At the time of a new moon, we cannot see the Moon at all. This is because the other side of the Moon, which we cannot see, is lit up.

crescent

As the Moon and the Earth turn, we can see part of the Moon that is lit up. This is called a crescent moon.

Each night we can see more and more of the Moon that is lit up, until we can see all of it. Then, night by night, it looks as if the Moon is getting smaller and smaller again, until it disappears at the next new moon.

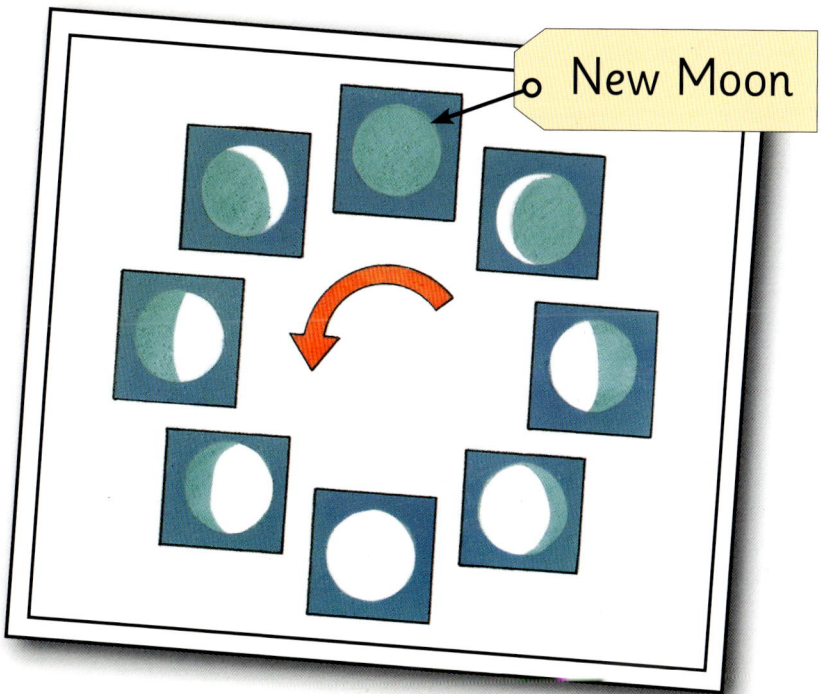

We say the Moon "waxes" as it gets bigger and "wanes" as it gets smaller.

Sometimes, as the Moon orbits the Earth, and the Earth orbits the Sun, they cross each other. The Moon, or the shadow of the Moon, can block out the Sun as they cross.

When this happens, it becomes dark. This is called an eclipse.

From the Earth, we always see the same side of the Moon. We never see the other side as it is always turned away from the Earth. This is because it takes the same time for the Moon to spin around as it takes for the Moon to orbit the Earth.

Despite being a long way away, the Moon does affect things on the Earth. As the Moon travels around, it attracts the Earth and its seas.

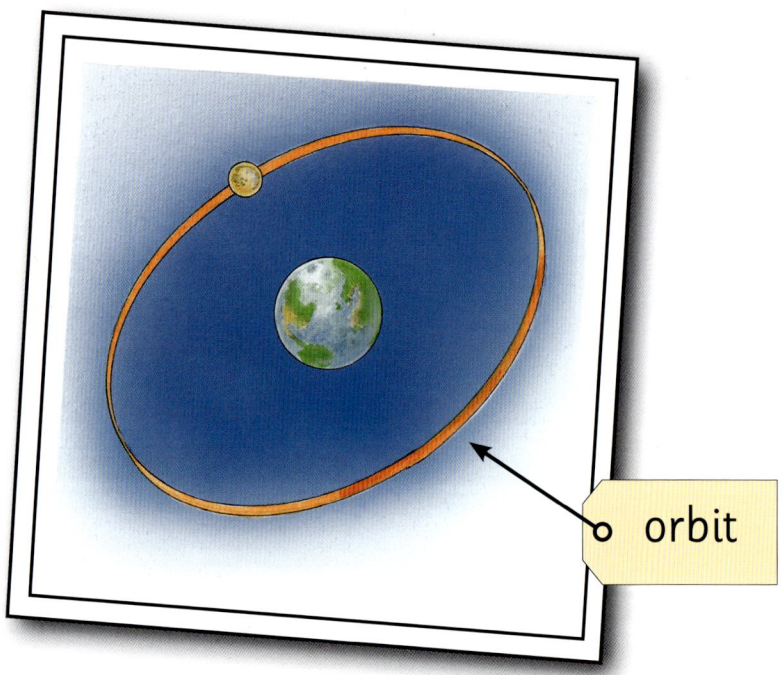

orbit

When the Moon is close to one part of the Earth, there is a high tide. As the Moon travels away, the sea levels fall and it is low tide.

We could not live on the Moon. It is rocky, dry and barren. The Moon's night is very, very cold and the Moon's day is very, very hot.

rocky

Man has always looked at the Moon and dreamed about visiting it.

Man first landed on the Moon in 1969. Six rockets have landed on the Moon and twelve men have walked on it. The gravity on the Moon is less than on the Earth. This is why, when you see someone walking on the Moon, they seem to jump and float along.

astronaut

rocket

The first rockets to go to the Moon were called Saturn rockets. Only a very small part of a rocket, the bit at the top, lands on the Moon. The rest of it is filled with fuel. It has three parts, and each part falls off as the fuel in it is used up.

When you look at the Moon with a telescope, you can see where rocks have crashed into it. The marks never get worn away as there is no weather on the Moon.

footprints

This means that the footprints left by the astronauts will still be there in thousands of years' time!